Properties of Materials

Comparing Properties

Charlotte Guillain

Heinemann Library
Chicago, Illinois

H **www.heinemannraintree.com**
Visit our website to find out
more information about
Heinemann-Raintree books.

To order:

☎ Phone 888-454-2279

🖱 Visit www.heinemannraintree.com
to browse our catalog and order online.

© 2009 Heinemann Library
an imprint of Capstone Global Library, LLC
Chicago, Illinois

Customer Service: 888-454-2279

Visit our website at www.heinemannraintree.com

Designed by Joanna Hinton-Malivoire
Photo research by Elizabeth Alexander
Printed and bound by Leo Paper Group

13 12 11 10 09
10 9 8 7 6 5 4 3 2 1

Library of Congress Cataloging-in-Publication Data
Guillain, Charlotte.
  Comparing properties / Charlotte Guillain.
    p. cm.
  Includes bibliographical references and index.
  ISBN 978-1-4329-3309-8 (hc) -- ISBN 978-1-4329-3310-4 (pb) 1.
Materials--Juvenile literature. I. Title.
  TA403.2.G85 2008
  620.1'12--dc22
                        2008055128

Acknowledgments
The author and publishers are grateful to the following for
permission to reproduce copyright material: Alamy pp. **5 left**
(© Andy Sutton), **5 right** (© Simon Rawles), **8, 12** (© Vario Images
GmbH & Co.KG), **10** (© Phil Degginger); © Capstone Publishers
pp. **18, 20 left and right** (Karon Dubke); Corbis p. **6** (© Adam
Woolfitt); iStockphoto p. **22 bottom right** (© Elena Schweitzer);
Photolibrary pp. **4 top left middle** (Glow Images), **16** (Fancy), **17**
(Philip Wilkins/Fresh Food Images), **19** (Brand X Pictures), **21 left**,
22 bottom left (Claver Carroll); Shutterstock pp. **4 top left**
(© Vladimir Mucibabic), **4 top right middle** (© Stephen Aaron Rees),
4 top right (© Yury Kosourov), **4 bottom middle, 22 top left** (©
Mike Flippo), **4 bottom left** (© Mario Lopes), **4 bottom right**
(© letty17), **7** (© GoodMood Photo), **9** (© Elena Elisseeva), **11** (© Tree
of Life), **13** (© Jasenka Lukša), **14** (© Dmitrijs Dmitrijevs), **15** (© Marc
Verdiesen), **21 right** (© Mindy W. M. Chung), **22 top middle** (© Ilike),
22 top right (© matka_Wariatka), **22 bottom middle** (© Cherick).

Cover photographs reproduced with permission of istockphoto: kites
(© Eric Michaud); istockphoto: icicles (© Erkki Makkonen); Alamy: a boat
(© Peter Blottman); istockphoto: boulders (© Zacarias Pereira da Mata);
Shutterstock: peeling paint (© ZTS); Shutterstock: a garden hose
(© dragon_fang); Shutterstock: a window (© Dana Bartekoske).

Back cover photograph reproduced with permission of Shutterstock:
an icicle (© Tree of Life).

Every effort has been made to contact copyright holders of any
material reproduced in this book. Any omissions will be rectified
in subsequent printings if notice is given to the publisher.

Some words appear in bold, **like this.** You can find out
what they mean in the "Words to Know" on page 23.

Contents

About this series
Each book in the Properties of Materials series introduces students to
the different properties of materials. Use this book to stimulate discussion
about comparing materials and ways to change the properties of materials.

What Are Materials?

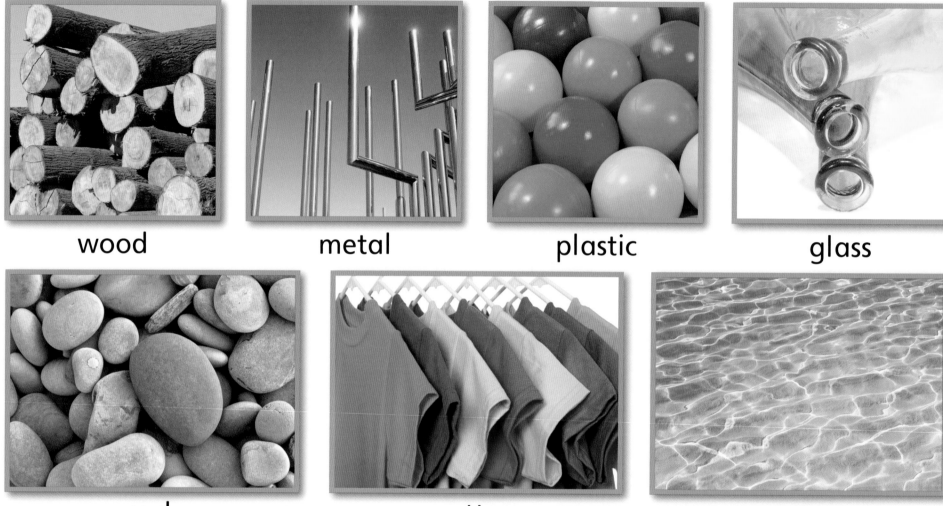

wood   metal   plastic   glass

rock   cotton   water

Wood, **metal**, plastic, and glass are all materials. Rock, cotton, and water are all materials.

hard   soft

Materials have many different **properties**. Materials can be hard or soft. The properties of a material are how it looks and feels.

Hard or Soft?

Materials can be hard or soft. Hard materials can be strong and heavy. Hard materials do not easily change shape.

Soft materials can be light and **stretchy**. Soft materials can change shape easily.

Heavy or Light?

Materials can be heavy or light. Heavy materials are hard to lift. Heavy things are often strong and **solid**.

Light materials are easy to lift. Light things are often not very strong.

Hot or Cold?

Materials can become hot or cold. When materials are hot they can change. When materials are hot they can become bright and **melt**.

When materials are cold they can change. When materials are cold they can become icy and hard.

Smooth or Rough?

Materials can be smooth or rough. Smooth materials can be flat. Smooth things have no bumps or cracks.

Rough materials can be bumpy or cracked. Rough materials do not feel flat under your fingers.

Shiny or Dull?

Materials can be **shiny** or dull. Shiny things **reflect** light so they can shine a lot. Shiny things are often smooth and hard.

Dull things do not reflect light very much. Dull things can be smooth or rough. Dull things can be hard or soft.

Stiff or Bendable?

Materials can be stiff or **bendable**. Stiff materials can be hard and they stay in one position. Stiff materials do not bend or stretch easily.

Bendable materials can bend and stretch. Bendable materials can be hard or soft.

Float or Sink?

hollow bottle

Materials can float or sink. Materials that float can be light, flat, or **hollow**. Some heavy things, such as big ships, can float. The water underneath pushes them up so they do not sink.

Materials that sink can be **solid** and heavy. Materials sink when they are heavy enough to push away the water underneath them.

Changing Materials

We can change materials in different ways. Materials can change shape when they become hot or cold. When we make things hot they can **melt**. When we make things cold they can **shrink** and become hard.

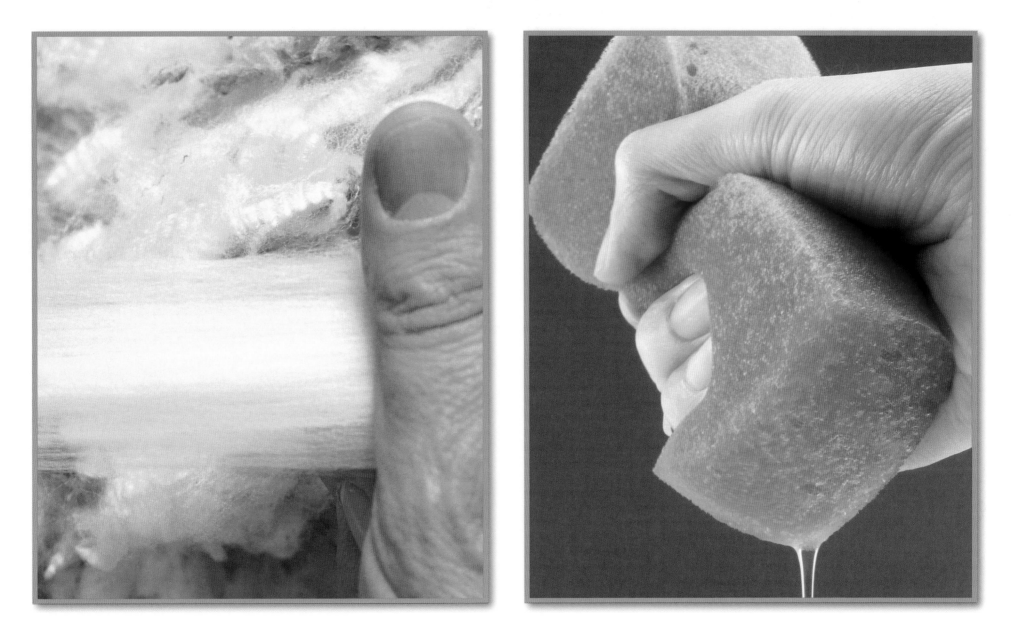

Materials can be changed by **forces**. Forces are pushes and pulls. When we bend, squeeze, or stretch materials we push and pull them.

Which Properties?

Which **properties** do these materials have?

Words to Know

bendable	material that can bend without breaking
force	a push or a pull
hollow	has an empty space inside it
melt	to become soft and runny when heated
metal	hard, shiny material
property	how a material looks and feels
reflect	material that light shines off. Mirrors reflect things.
shiny	bright
shrink	get smaller
solid	fixed shape that is not a gas or a liquid
stretchy	able to become longer or wider when pulled

Index

Note to Parents and Teachers

Before Reading

Tell children that materials have many different properties. Explain to children that properties are how materials look and feel. As children give examples of properties, create a chart titled "Properties of Materials." The chart should have two columns: "Materials Can Look" and "Materials Can Feel." After the chart is created, hold up pictures of different types of materials. Have children describe the pictures by using words they created from the chart.

After Reading

1. Place children in small groups with boxes of objects. The children should sort the objects by their properties. Walk around and have the children explain why they placed the objects in specific groups. As groups are finishing, the boxes can be rotated around the room until each group has sorted each box.

2. Children can go on a hunt around the room or outside for materials with specific properties (e.g., hard, soft, rough, shiny, dull, hot, cold, or stiff). Give children five minutes to look for one property at a time. They have to record their objects on a piece of paper. Whoever finds the most objects wins!